DIVINE
EXPLORATIONS &
Moon Soul
MUSINGS

A POETIC WANDERING
ALONG THE RIVER

ISBN-13: 978-0692809136 (IbbiLane Press)
ISBN-10: 0692809139

IBBILANEPRESS.COM

IbbiLane

PRESS

Foreword

This book, "Divine Explorations and Moon Soul Musings...A Poetic Wandering Along the River" makes consistent discoveries of empowerment. The poet and the poem are one, making observations through her spiritual eyes, and conveying them with her gifts of writing and teaching skills. Jody Doty is a writer, minister, healer, spiritual guide, and has an intuitive consciousness. You, as the reader of this book, will experience all these wonderful attributes by just engaging yourself in Jody's spiritual writings.

I first met Jody on Facebook and grew to love her writings which I found poignant and helpful to many aspects of my life. Her applications to life gave causes to the reality of truth and the spiritual principles that she abides by. The content of this book is from a divine source where the words are the cornerstone to any action you want to take to improve, protect, comfort, and be inspired. Jody is the connection needed in every aspect of your life. For instance, Finding your way, it is not, a way, but your way, and it is not just worded in a book, here you will learn how the journey becomes the way of your heart.

The author's divine revelation accompanies you through specific readings of enlightenment to be used as guides in assisting you on your journey through life. They are more than devotions and meditations. They are declarations of who you really are.

Robert S. Hayes BA. Bed, Author-Poet
Retired Math and Science Teacher
Published Math and Science texts

Preface

This book is proof positive that dreams come true and I mean this quite literally. I had a vision one amazing evening six months ago after making the leap between mundane midnight musings and a replay of my daily activities mixed with wishful wanting about the future. It was then that I drifted quite purposefully into this poetic creation of heavenly inspired words that spilled forth from my cosmic consciousness. There I was in the middle of my sleepy dream holding this book entitled "Divine Explorations and Moon Soul Musings...a Poetic Wandering Along the River." It was at that moment that I realized a book of my prose, poems and musings had already written itself in spirit. I merely needed to let my body get on board so the book could write itself into reality.

My writings are inspired through daily meditation and connection with the divine. The words pour through me like beautiful gifts from heaven. Although some are personal in nature, I believe all of the writings were meant to be shared as they contain a thread of universal truth that may touch the heart, lift the spirit and light a path of hope, inspiration and healing. Among the prose, poetry and musings shared, are some pieces I affectionately call "soul writings." These are "divined" descriptions of a specific individual's soul essence for which I have utilized my spiritual gift of clear sight (clairvoyance) to tune into their soul's inner beauty, traits, emotions, symbols and other spiritual qualities they present in the world. For many of the soul writings, I have provided first name dedications with much love and gratitude for the request to do the soul writing and for the permission to share it publicly.

Finally, for those who believe they are too old to write a book or share their unique gifts in this world, I am here to say it is never too late. I have been writing less than a year and a half and I'm in my late 50's. It began when I meditated on the word "creativity." As soon as I released limitations to what it means to be creative, the words simply came. When your dreams, passion and creativity collide, it is your time to shine. Many blessings to you on this journey called life.

Jody Doty

Dedication

I dedicate this book to anyone who has a dream and the courage to work through fear, doubt and pain to make it happen. We are all dreamers in this world meant to polish and shine our soul, to share our unique and beautiful gifts in the brightest way possible. I encourage you to find the magic within, to tap into your divinity and to bravely and joyfully enter the place where hope, creativity and action meet to make your "happily ever after's" come true.

To my parents, Barbara and Paul Rentner; my husband, Dave; children, Megan and Jason, family members and friends who have encouraged me to share this amazing gift from heaven, the beautiful words that flow through me, I thank you from the deepest place in my heart and soul.

To my poet and writer friends, your words of validation, support and kindred calling mean so much to me and I dedicate this book to you and all of those who are fortunate enough to experience and are moved by your amazing gift of prose and poetry. Special thank you to my incredibly talented poet friend, Robert Hayes, for your support and kind words shared here.

To my artist and musician friends, pictures, art and music speak a universal language. For your time and dedication to your craft and the joy you bring, I thank you. The combination of a poet's dreamy words and the beauty of art, photography and music is an incredible, creative gift to our world.

To my spiritual teachers, coaches, counselors and friends, you are my tribe. You hold my hand and my heart; you help bring out the best in me. You enlighten, encourage, prod and keep things real. You lift me up and catch me when I fall. Thank you for being there in body and spirit and for sharing your gifts of love and healing. This includes you, Kellie Fitzgerald, my soul sister, encourager and publisher of the book. You are all keepers.

Special shout out to Barb & Paul, Dave, Jason, Megan, Tracy, Rochelle, Linda, Kellie, Leah, Mary Ellen, Danny, Ana, Valerie, Alana, Faith, Barb E, Victoria, Cheryl, Patti, Paula, Jeanne, Brenda, Kathy, Sandi, Carol, Jacki, Connie, Chris, Akiko, Katie, Harvey, Cindy, Peter, Wendy, Florise, Pat, Meg, Jodi and Portia.

Table of Contents

I

River Birth

Recollection

She went about collecting pieces of her soul that were lost, taken, and scattered about the universe until at last she became whole, a beautiful mosaic of self-love and forgiveness. With that, she began the next chapter in the masterpiece that is her life.

PIER INTO SELF

Park yourself on the pier and dip
your toes into the river. Let the
water baptize your feet sending a
cool, satisfying healing to your
soul. Pause and reflect on your
purpose, what you want to
accomplish, how far you've come
and how amazing you are.
Bookmark this moment on the
timeline of your soul as a loving
reference for later when you need
a peaceful reminder that being
here is a beautiful gift and you
make a magnificent ripple
in the river of life.

TIMELY TUMBLE

She ran full tilt in the direction
of her dreams, tripped and fell
joyfully into her soul in a timely
tumble of personal truth,
a serendipitous spill of passionate
proportion. She finally landed in a
state of grace, kissed the ground of
her being, and rose like the sun
embracing the dawn
of her new beginning.

BEGINNER

The path ahead is unclear.
There will always be unanticipated
challenges, bumps in the road,
learning curves and dead ends.
Regardless, I stand at a crossroad.
I cannot go back. I've already been
there. I must bravely take that first
step, the one that will lead me to
my new tomorrow. The journey is
mine. Let me begin it with courage.
Let me wrap my faith around my
shoulders like a shawl, and walk
into the unknown, recalling the
excitement of what it's like to be
a beginner. This is the song of my
soul, the voice that spurs me
onward, prompting me to rise from
complacency, to risk uncertainty,
and to walk with an open heart
remembering my place
in the dream.

LIFE'S BACKPACK

Don't view this as an ending.
Instead, see it as an opening, an
opportunity to take your life off
hold and begin a new chapter.
This is the time to do those things
you were not able to accomplish
because you were tied to the past,
to a relationship, to an expectation.
Release the pain and welcome the
infusion of you. Fill your body with
self-love and awaken your soul.
Starting over is like kindergarten.
Put on your life's backpack and
welcome new learning, new
relationships, new excitement on
this, the first day of your journey.

THE PATH OF THE SOUL

Sometimes my soul's path is beautifully illuminated, clearly marked and easy to skip down. Other times it's overgrown with challenge, causes me to trip and is in need of spiritual weed whacking. The purpose of the path is unchanged. It's my faith, attention and intention that make the difference on the journey.

THE FLOW

The river doesn't judge. It simply keeps moving, changing, patiently carving its path in companion with the elements. Attune with the river of your life. Freely make your way. Trust the flow and persevere with passionate resilience.

II

Sun, Moon and Divinity

MOON SOUL

She has dreams of freedom locked deep within her soul. What is it that troubles her so that she can't break through her endless thoughts, excuses, reasons, busyness and fear to get to the heart of home? She has run away so often that she scarcely remembers the way, let alone her password of purpose. She needs to place her mind on a time out, to lovingly turn her thoughts and worries over to her daytime angels, so her evening self can have some peace, some solitude, a time to rest, to sigh, to dream, to be. Slow down little Miss. Let your tired body slumber. There are stars to see, angels to visit, and your moon soul to love.

SWEET DREAMS

Open your heart. Send a beam of love and faith toward heaven. Ask for angels to wrap you in their timeless love. Feel their protective countenance and release any fear or worries to them. Invite your highest vibration of peace to fill your heart and gently flow into every cell of your body. Remember that even in the darkest times you are never alone in this world. You are lovingly held in divine grace. You need only ask to receive support. Take time to breathe in love and breathe out fear. Remind yourself that you are both a blessing and blessed as you close your weary eyes and let your body rest on a pillow of heavenly peace. Sweet dreams.

SMILING AT THE MOON

Somehow we just can't help smiling at the moon because in our small way we know there is connection, something quite powerful at play, as if another world is drawing us into its mystery, its magic and the grandeur of love's illumination in lunar form.

SACRED INVITATION

I am called to simply walk, to suspend all thought, to surrender doubt and scatter indecision to the setting sun. My body moves in companion with the wind, my feet comforted by the soothing wet sand, my breath mesmerized, attuning with the rhythm of timeless river ripples. Clarity settles in and with it comes a gentle peace, a subtle welcoming as if my soul has been gifted a sacred invitation to attend the cosmic dance that is night.

ANGELS

Please, he begged, won't you
tell me everything there is to
know about heaven and angels?
Oh, my dear, you must know
those answers lie deep within
your heart, wrapped lovingly
around your soul, and are truly
beyond question. Some things
just are. Believe.

I LIT
A CANDLE

I lit a candle for peaceful
understanding, its flame a
symbol of a soul's search for
light in the vast darkness of
anger, violence, and hatred. I lit
a candle for awareness, a simple
offering of warmth to a world
thrust in the coldness of
discontent. I lit a candle for
innocence, for eyes to radiate
their pure light of loving
kindness. I lit a candle for words
with the power and wisdom to
affect clarity, communion and
civility. I lit a candle for
forgiveness, for empathy, for
resurrecting that which has
been destroyed. I lit a candle for
love to sustain us, divinity to
guide us, and peace to grace
our soul, our home, our world.
I lit a candle.

FAITH

When I don't know for sure,
faith drops by for a visit. Ours
is a sacred bond, an invisible
friendship that restores my
belief that love's magic is
happening every moment
if we simply believe.

MYSTIC
OF THE
MOONLIGHT

I'm a mystic of the moonlight
shining my magic in the dark
of night, lighting a path of joy
to the welcoming stars.

EVENING'S GRACE

I spread my tender wings and fly my
soul into the heart of evening's
grace. It is here, in the light of love,
that I am home.

LILY

In my late night imagining, I land
lightly on a lily, a magical wisp of
wonder, eyes bright like a dragonfly,
a human fairy who wants nothing
more than to hug the twinkling stars
and dance into the welcome sigh
of a moonlit dream.

DANDELION DREAMS

Be like the dandelion. Share yourself in the world. Go with the flow and bring joy to those who pick you. Assure them they, too, can make a wish and blow it into the universe. Be with them to watch their dreams take flight on winds of faith, land on opportunity, and multiply in love.

RAINBOWS AND FLOWERS

My heart speaks in rainbows and flowers. Nature is my prayer, stirs my soul, grounds my being and brings out the very best in me.

NIGHT SHADE

I'm not afraid of the dark. I like to think of it as God pulling down a magnificent night shade of peace and wrapping me in a blanket of love so that my body may rest and my soul can dance in heaven's ether creating beautiful dreams to come.

GARDEN OF TWILIGHT

It's time to rest, to leave the garden of twilight and retreat to the world of blissful sleep with only the moon to watch over you and angels to sing peaceful lullabies while you dream of brand new dawns to come.

CASTING WISHES

Let me remember to work in companion with my spirit and not fight the process or try to control situations. I shall cast my net of wishes into life's river and invite a bounty of divine joy to return as it is meant to with as much grace and abundance as my body can hold.

BESTIES

The moon and I are besties. We understand the beauty in the stillness of the dark, but we choose to shine because life is all about illumination.

THE MOON STILL SHINES

Despite it all the moon still shines like a night light in the dark sky. The ocean waves do their best to gently wash away yesterday's troubles, sifting, releasing and purging, until there is nothing left but the purity of earth, well-loved sand. Hold tight to the knowledge that a brand new day is coming. You are like the sand. Let the troubles of the day purge from your body. Lovingly release them to the angels. Bless your heart and let peace fill your soul.

III

Earth, Sky, Water
and *the Seasons*

GOLDEN SOUL OF AUTUMN

She's the golden soul of autumn, a radiant free-fall of purposeful passion tossed about in the breeze of unpredictability that is her life. Content despite the chaos, she's a messenger of hopeful changeability seasoned in feminine splendor, a colorful gift of the spirit wherever she happens to land.

RAIN OF MY SOUL

Life can rain buckets. Some may
think this is a drenching of the
soul, but I view it as a
quintessential quenching, a fluid
invitation of my emotions to match
the weather of my moment. While
often sunny, with a few puffy
clouds thrown in for fun, there are
times during fall's northwest rain
squalls that I imagine everything I
want or need to release and purge
from my life is pooled into a
beautiful waterfall of gratitude.
Thankful for the time and place
they served, I lovingly release old
feelings and memories as a
refreshing downpour, images
purposefully washed away by the
grace of nature until I'm
resplendently refreshed in the
glory of all that remains, that which
is permanent, revealed and true,
the forever place
of new beginnings.

SACRED STILLNESS

And in the sacred stillness of its night, the world felt the many prayers for peace and twinkled in gratitude.

BLANKET OF SKY

And the world wrapped its heavenly night sky blanket around them, stars and all, tucking them in and reminding them how much they are loved.

WINTER SKY

And in that sacred moment of peaceful release, the winter sky opened its watchful eye and blanketed the horizon with thousands of frozen tears filled with white joy for all the world to behold.

SPELLBOUND

And then suddenly snowflakes of peace floated over the area and a winter white calm settled in holding its captives spellbound and gloriously home bound for a time.

SPRINGTIME

After the rain come the flowers. Let the spring of your life remind you of renewal, of your beauty bursting through the darkness, the mud, the hardships. Open your heart and bloom your soul brightly in this world. Splash, play and laugh remembering the simple joys of life. Appreciate how far you've come and bookmark the now of springtime.

DREAMER'S HEART

In my dreamer's heart, I'd like to think the stars wish upon us too.

RIPPLE

Your love is a ripple on the river of
my soul, your eyes the sparkling
sunrise lighting my way, your body
an elegant tree gracing the shore
of my being, casting its shadow of
heavenly beauty that melds
completely with the twilight
of my waking dreams.

MERMAID

She's a mermaid it would seem.
Her heart belongs to the sun and
moon. Her emotions are tied to the
water that sustains her. She's
beautifully unique, a combination
of fluid femininity and watery
whimsy. Deeply spiritual, she's an
intuitive with a heart of gold
and a shimmering soul.

WATER SPIRIT

I'm the spirit of the water. I want to feel the river of life around me, to dip in and out of my moments with freedom and joy, to swim effortlessly between worlds, to welcome the grace of the day and bless the night, to warm my soul in the sun and wash me whole in the quiet of the moonlight.

PONDERING STILLNESS

To sit and ponder by the stillness of the water, to gaze into the blue of the sky, to immerse myself in the grand mystery of nature, this is my awakening, my amazing grace, my breath of heaven on Earth.

LAGOON

You are the lagoon of my memory,
clutching me in the tangle of your
mesmerizing muck, the muddiness
of you. I'm captive to the pull,
submerged in vague sadness, my
feelings waterlogged and murky.
Time suffocating the breath of us
in an old familiar heartache.
Surrender me once more to the
depths of love like a lonesome lily
destined to float unconsciously
in the pooled silence
of what used to be.

CONTEMPLATING CLOUDS

I remember when I was a child lying in a field of clover on a hot Midwest day and looking up at the blue sky and the puffy cotton ball clouds and trying to imagine what images I was meant to see in the clouds as they floated by. It was an innocent time, a time of wonder at the vastness of nature, the beauty of the world, the simplicity of peaceful contemplation, the honoring of a child's curious imagination. It should be no different as an adult. We complicate things so. Love is simple. Dream it, express it, do it, be it, and don't forget to contemplate the clouds.

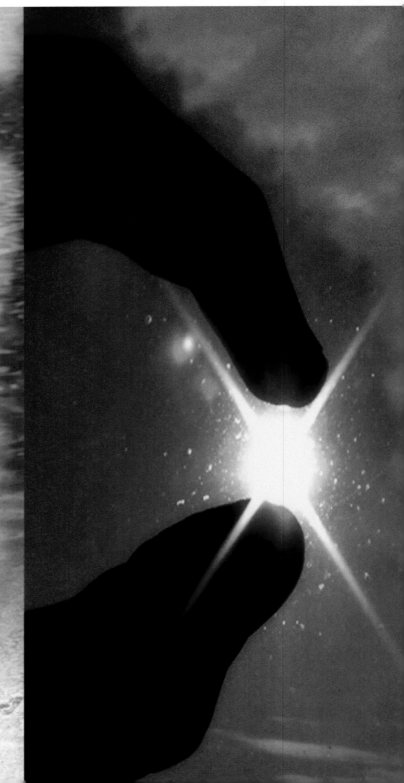

SKY WRITING

Her soul content, she smiled
releasing her words like butterflies
to the universe, knowing they
would be gathered by angels and
shared like shining stars in the
night sky, literary sprinkles of
enchantment and magic, destined
for lovers and dreamers
to wish upon.

THE ROCKY PATH

Sometimes the path is rocky.
Consider the cracks as courage
and the stones are strength
as you bravely press onward.

CONNECT THE DOTS

Sometimes
all she wants to do
is play connect the dots
with the stars.

SKY OF MYSTERY

After all we've been through during our day, we are often blessed with the gift of beautiful shining stars in a sky of mystery. We stand like children in awe, taking their presence on faith, accepting that stars are there without our effort, our control, our judgment. They merely shine their light, inviting us to dream, to believe, to love just because. We are no less and can be so much more.

COMING IN FOR A LANDING

Sometimes it's good to stop flying, to rest your wings, to land, to look upon the world as an observer, to see with new eyes, to feel, sense and know the moment, to settle into you, to sift and grasp the grand alchemy of sky, water, and Earth, to be home, to gain perspective, to value the center, the crossroad of your journey, until once again you are called to rise with renewed wings of awareness and lovingly soar your reawakened soul.

EPIPHANY

And then suddenly peace descended upon her, as if a thousand doves became one and found their way home to her lost, scattered soul. She immersed herself in a moonlit dance of radiant purity, joyfully accepting this timely and timeless baptism of her soul. The evening stars applauded her homecoming and she shimmered and bowed in the divine spotlight of this holy night.

HOME

I am the water, the shore, the
sun, the moon, the wind and
the rain. I am integral to all that
is and carry this beautiful truth
within my heart, feel it in my
breath and know it in my soul.
It resonates in my waking
moments and I dream of it
eternally when I'm called
home to remember.

IV

Nature, Plants & Animals

Glen in the Woods

Give me a glen in the woods, a garden of ground and magnificent butterfly wings of whimsy and I'll bank off my dreams and soar my soul like the enchanted gypsy goddess that I am.

TREES OF MY WINDOW

What glorious joy to wake to
singing birds, to sense daybreak
through the trees of my window, to
stretch my restless body in time to
morning's rhythm, to try to fathom
anything more beautiful than
welcoming the awakening
of a new day.

WILDFLOWER WALTZ

Oh please invite me to waltz among the
wildflowers, take a serendipitous spin with
my garden friends. Dress them in colorful
petals and sensible roots. Let them fill my
dance card with fun, nourish the ground of
my being, quench my thirst for beauty and
resonate in reverence with the flowering
radiance of my blooming soul.

KINDNESS IS A BUTTERFLY

Kindness is a butterfly gently floating above life's flowers spreading its light-filled colorful wings while exuding a tender beauty that livens and enriches our world. As it lands, it captivates us, lifting our spirits, inviting our attention and smiles, for a moment suspending time in a magical wonderland of gentle beauty and appreciation. The butterfly, a transformer; kindness a life changer, welcome visitors to nature, human and garden. It's no wonder our loved ones are believed to visit us in the form of an angelic butterfly, body changed in form but oh so stunning in ethereal beauty. It's God's sharing of an eternal kindness.

RAINMAKER OF MY DREAMS

It is stormy outside, furious wind, driving rain, restless trees, grays and blues of a mutable sky, simultaneously confused and certain. It is not unlike the stirring and sifting of my soul, the torrential push to match the transforming power of nature's call for change. Sometimes transition is in stillness, in the quiet calm of certainty, in the gentleness of knowing. Other times I'm moved by the power of life's fierce storm, pushing me with the strength of passionate purpose to pay attention to all of the elements, what needs focus, how to change, what is this season of emotions. Let me go with the storm, surrender my soul to solutions, shift my thoughts, surf my challenges, move my potential out of complacency and into the power of action, the world of doing, of being the rainmaker of my dreams, bursting forth as a whirlwind of soulful power, a breeze of love making the old and tired new again, undeniably alive. Vibrantly blow away the dying leaves of my past and hollow a place within to sprout me, water me, renew my life. Grow my soul in swells and squalls of serendipity so saturated in clarity that I can't help but shed my spiritual raincoat of protection and stand in the gale of delight until the storm passes and I am forever changed and once again called to bask in the silence of more to be.

MOTHER OCEAN

Meanwhile, as the human children slept cozy in their beds, the soul of mother ocean tucked in her nautical kids, wrapping them in waves of watery love, holding them close to her heart in peaceful harmony under a starlit evening sky, inviting each to make a splendid splash of serendipity and find their special place in the twilight hours of dream time.

FIRE STORM

There's an imminent flame burning in this passionate soul of mine. It's seizing hold, igniting desire's kindling in a fire storm that will surely burn through the superfluous, the dry forest of doubt, destroying fear's illusion and searing its way through to the heart of love, a cinder of smoldering clarity matched by the illumination of my newly awakened destiny.

NIGHT OWL

She's an evening gal, a bird of the night, an owl maiden, sharing her loneliness with a still listening moon. Her friends call her wise one, advice giver, relationship whisperer, but her own lover's nest is empty and her wisdom eludes her. In a rare moment of introspection, she finally cries out to the moon, "Who, who am I?" The trees offer comfort as the dawn of her day breaks through. In the light of the morning sun, she gently drifts to sleep with renewed hope in her heart. "I'm so glad you finally asked," replied the universe with a knowing smile as it gently whispered the answers to her welcoming soul.

YOU AND ME

He was chocolate, chocolate chip with a tablespoon of peanut butter for good measure. She was spumoni, colorful and fruity. Their tastes quite different, but in the end they melted just the same.

HOPE

And in the distance, beyond the clouds, just past life's rainbow, look for hope. It is our life's umbrella, the invisible force that spurs us on when heavy emotions pour through us and dampen our spirits. Let the resiliency of hope move you out of the darkness of your difficulties and into its loving light. Hope heralds change and invites new opportunities to strengthen resolve and grow your soul.

MAGIC OF YOU

It's only a matter of time, a period of healing, a moment of fate and faith colliding in joyous reunion that stands between you and connecting with the beauty of your light within. In the meantime, the magic that is your soul waits patiently for your rediscovery and surrender to self-love.

GARDEN ANGEL

And in a moment of blissful
transformation, angels descended
from heaven on wings of doves and
held her tenderly in their loving
embrace, filling her doubtful soul
with eternal love, and reminding her
that she is exquisite as she is, a
beautiful synthesis of starlight and
form, meant to shimmer and bloom,
a human flower in God's
garden of Earth

FREEDOM IN YOUR SOUL

Be like a bird with freedom in your soul, prayers beneath your wings and a voice that sings in joyful gratitude for another day of living.

POND OF HER DREAMS

And the princess loved him just the way he is, a beautiful frog in the pond of her dreams.

HUMAN TREE *for Cheryl*

While walking in the woods close to my home, it occurred to me that one of my favorite teachers inspires me by its mere presence on the planet. It does not speak in words, but has a universal language that resonates with each soul it encounters. Blessed are our trees, nature's enduring gift.

Trees teach us to be rooted, to be present, grounded in our being and fully connected with our soul. They are a green, living timeline, a reminder that that we are always growing, spreading our limbs, and reaching upward toward to the sky.

Trees illustrate the gift of generosity, of unconditional sharing and giving. They provide us shelter, comfort, shade, warmth, and food. They encourage our resilience during trying times, inspiring us to hold strong and weather life's storms. Trees remind us that we, too, are beautiful beings, self-sufficient in our individuality and quite powerful when we unite as a group, a human forest.

Trees are accepting of other creatures in our world. Unprejudiced, they happily share themselves with birds, squirrels, chipmunks, owls, and raccoons. Trees provide us a tranquil place for reflection and meditation, a sturdy wooden foundation for reading a book or painting a picture on a sunny afternoon.

On days when I am feeling stressed, overwhelmed, or out of sync with life, I love to stand in the woods, feel the earth beneath my feet, the wind in my hair, and imagine that I am a human tree, grounded, strong, beautiful, resilient, comforting, accepting and receptive, living my life fully, growing my soul.

V

Human
Element

FROLIC

He's a bit unusual, a gentle lamb that stands out in the flock. He gets it that the world can be a harsh place for someone so sensitive, but this does not deter him from being his happy-go-lucky authentic self. He prefers to feel the world with his heart, to admire the beauty of transformation in a butterfly and to dance his soul in a fearless frolic among the flowers.

TRUCE

The woman she is recalls the innocent little girl inside, the one who took in life with big brown eyes of wonder, who doubted people but never God, the girl who rescued strays and prayed for baby birds that fell out of the nest, the one who fancied herself a real live Alice in Wonderland, convinced flowers have souls and nature erupts in symphonic sound. The woman remembers the girl's excitement about fall colors, and new pencils, dancing, the first blush of romance, the desire for perfection and the realization it doesn't exist. The girl child is restless, bored, tired of sharing herself with an adult body steeped in dutiful responsibility. Today they call a truce, join forces and meld the best of both, enthusiasm and wisdom, playful imagination and practicality. Integration and wholeness are amazing gifts the woman thinks to herself as she puts down the laundry, imagines her life is hopscotch, throws a magic rock and skips with joy at the prospect of a new day.

THE LEDGE

I sat quietly on the ledge of my life, peering over the edge into what seemed like an eternity, but really it was only a glimpse of my moments. That's when I welcomed my soul's wings and flew gently into the vastness of my dreams.

SHE GOES DEEP

And she goes deep, to the quiet place where tears meet the heart and dreams seem miles away. Yet, she knows intuitively that her life is taking a turn if she can just hang on past this moment. Hers is the spirit of a horse, mane flying, instincts kicking in and running full tilt into the promise of her new life, her soon to be realized reality. For now, she can feel the wind, see the landscape ahead and taste the freedom in her soul

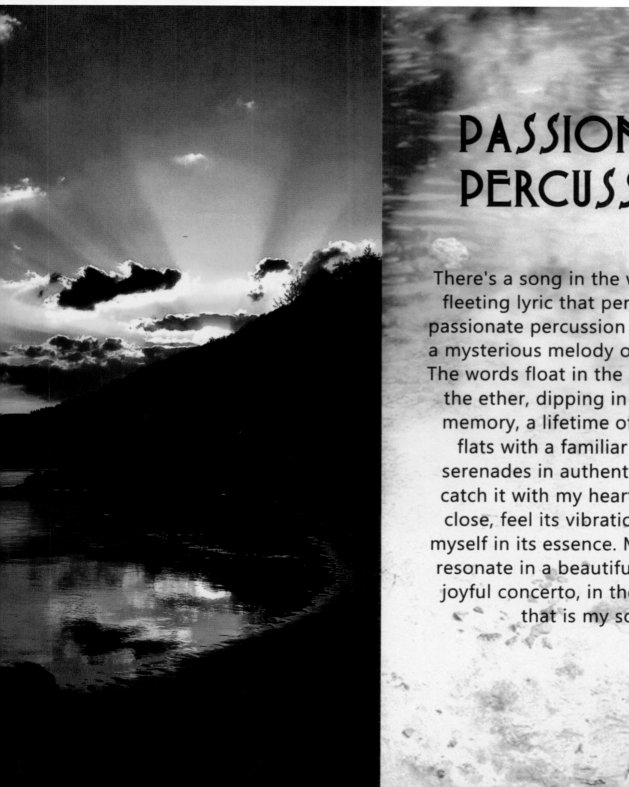

PASSIONATE PERCUSSION

There's a song in the wind, a lilting fleeting lyric that percolates with passionate percussion and murmurs a mysterious melody of melancholy. The words float in the serendipity of the ether, dipping in and out my memory, a lifetime of sharps and flats with a familiar voice that serenades in authenticity. Let me catch it with my heart and hold it close, feel its vibration and wrap myself in its essence. May it forever resonate in a beautiful sonata, the joyful concerto, in the symphony that is my soul.

ON BEAUTY

Her beauty is a verb with vibe. Her eyes sparkle starlight. Her heart beats compassion. Her feet dance in companion with the angelic aria of her singing soul. Her voice whispers in windy harmonics while her skin synthesizes the sweet softness of simplicity and the sadness of scars. Her hair highlights the passing of time while her healing hands write her untold story. From the fortress of the body into the welcoming world, the luminescence of eternal beauty always shines through.

HOPE FILLED HEART

And then ever so tenderly she held her hope-filled heart in her hand and began a new love affair with her life.

TWILIGHT SEDUCTRESS

There's something soothingly
seductive about the moon with
its sliver of lulling light in the
dark doubt of the world, an
evening invitation to stir the
sleepless soul, conjuring
mystical memories, sprinkles of
stardust and flashes of twilight
intuition, a magical awakening,
the hopeful summoning of long
forgotten dreams from the day.

THE OLD FARMHOUSE

There's something about an old farmhouse sitting alone in an open field with a few shade trees that inspires and makes me smile. Perhaps it's my Midwest roots or my love of nature's land and heaven's sky meeting at early dawn and colorful dusk. There's a certain comfort in knowing the house has survived many cold winters and sweltering summers and yet remains steadfast and sturdy, a little worn but unpretentious in its welcoming beauty. I can just imagine the warmth provided generations of family and the kids and grandkids who enjoyed playing on the sunny porch or singing happily in the old tire swing. As I grow older, I can relate to the Mom-like quality the farmhouse exudes, its strength, resilience and caring comfort, its peaceful quiet filled with memories. When I pass from this Earth, I hope to be like an old farmhouse, extending my welcoming soul into the arms of God and watching the light of my being as it joins in an exquisite moment of sunrise in spirit and sunset in body, to forever be an eternal porch light and symbol of the way home.

SUNFLOWER AMONG THE ROSES

She's convinced she's nothing special in her faded jeans, an old plaid shirt, and a well-worn scrunchie in her morning crazy hair. She's a "low maintenance, no frills, no fuss, no makeup" kind of gal with nothing to hide. She doesn't realize she's stunning in her simplicity, gorgeous in her genuineness, a radiant sunflower among the roses, and that's her real beauty. She just is.

CHILDHOOD TAKE TWO

In her dreams, she longs for a second chance at childhood lost, to forever erase the dark images that surface each night when her head hits the pillow. She tries to forget that in her world bedtime was a scary proposition that left little doubt the Boogeyman was real and lived with her.

This time is different. This time she'll experience what it's like to feel safe in her own skin, to be free to be who she is, to not hold her breath or shut her eyes. In her do-over world, she will speak fearlessly from her heart and live each day without regret, guilt and shame. She is ready to relinquish her role as "keeper of the family secrets," to live life honestly in loving kindness. This new home of her dreams has boundaries and respects her personal space.

She's ready to bravely open the door of forgiveness. She's done the work, healed her soul. There is nothing left to do but pack up her pain and leave her past behind. She smiles knowing it's never too late to love the child within her heart, to play, to color, to read stories, to create with clay, to snuggle a teddy bear. She's all about second chances and why not? It's a new day and she has the power to make her dreams come true.

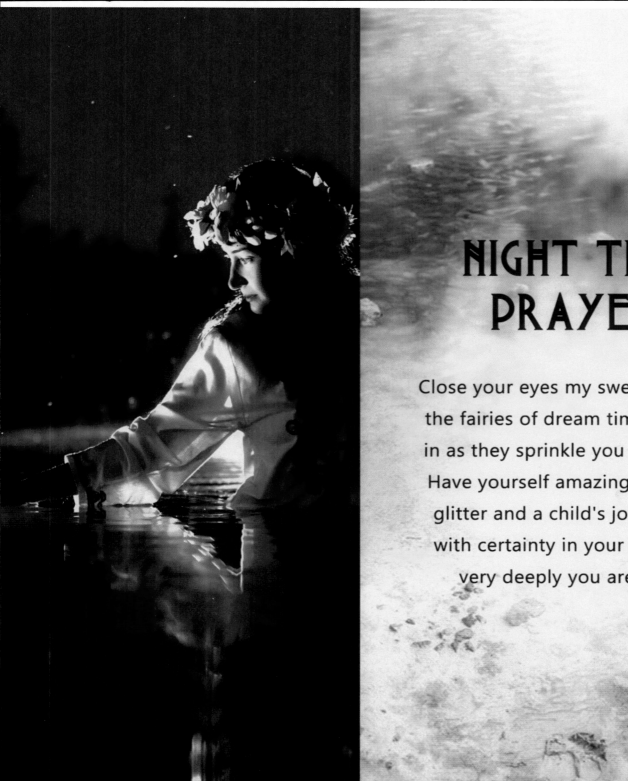

NIGHT TIME PRAYER

Close your eyes my sweet child. Let
the fairies of dream time tuck you
in as they sprinkle you in stardust.
Have yourself amazing dreams of
glitter and a child's joy knowing
with certainty in your heart how
very deeply you are loved.

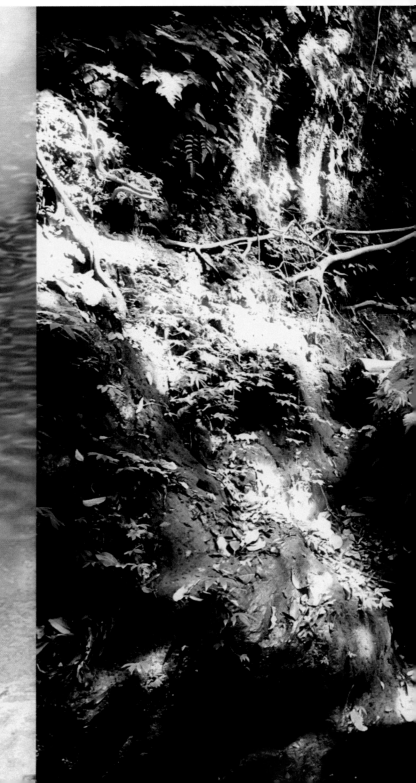

PRELUDE TO A DREAM

Take me to the place of imagination, of longing and limitless creation and beautiful anticipation, the prelude to the dream. Let my soul spur me onward until my body is ready to fly.

SOUL SEARCH

Most folks will show you their cover, a preferred page or passage, perhaps a periodic autobiography with favored fact or frivolous fiction. But a seeker, a lover, an artist, a philosopher will delve deeper, beyond the confines of the consensus container, the makeshift mask of perception, to the beauty of imperfection, the meat of mystery, the one page, paragraph, line, and word that reveals the truth, the essence, the soul's story, and then tenderly read it by heart.

ONE GUST AT A TIME
for Alana

She's an amazing woman-child, a bundle of endless potential in a vulnerable shell, a blazing stick of dynamite in a glass jar. She's wise beyond her years and yet equally fragile. She's lived a lifetime already, but still navigates the world of emotions. Anxious to live her dreams, there is no doubt she was born to change this world. For now, help her to remember that while she's trying so hard and fast to spread her wings and fly, she's still growing and learning, an energetic nestling who doesn't quite have all of her feathers. They are coming. Her courage, charisma and strength are admirable, but wisdom also calls for her to reach out to those who love her, to feel their uplifting support under her wings as she launches. Life is a long course, a process of lift offs and touch and go's. Watch over her with grace while she gently flaps and glides. She'll be soaring sky high in no time. After all, the universe is hers one gust at a time.

CASTING TO THE WIND

There's something emotionally freeing about casting my thoughts of you to the wind and watching them fly like a bird. You landed on the rock of my life for a reason. Yet now I wish to stand firmly on my own, to make this world mine and embrace independence. I won't forget how you changed my life; my prayer for you is that the wind lead you to a place of love and forgiveness. For me, I am a woman at peace. There's an river of opportunity before me and I'm ready to swim.

BLISSFUL SLEEP

I'm longing for blissful sleep, to lie my head on the pillow and drift off with the sandman and angels to adventures in the ether. What a touch of sweet awakening to have the morning greeting be one that is rested and refreshed. My friend, sleep, find me once more. Take me where you are. Heal my weariness with your restorative magic.

It is my dream.

KEEPER OF THE TEARS
for Portia

She's a sweet soul healing others with her glorious smile. A compassionate, sensitive girl, she feels deeply and sheds a waterfall of tears for those in need, who are hurting, lost or abandoned. She gives of herself freely and genuinely from the heart. But now her well is dry. Her body is tired. Her heart guarded. She has been strong for others, but she feels weak. A giver who has over-given at the expense of her own happiness and freedom. It's time for her to stop doing, to be still, to breathe. She needs to adjust her priorities, make a date with herself, rediscover what it's like to receive, to let the tears flow, to be vulnerable, receptive, to put her own well-being at the top of her "to do" list. She must open her heart and fill it with her loving essence, to light her internal candle and shine from within, filling her dark corners with her highest vibration of self. Heal the healer starting today.

CHILD OF NATURE
for Jason

He is a gentle soul, a sensitive child of nature, at home playing in the woods, listening to crickets, watching the color of the sky change like magic before him. He is wise beyond his years, feels the pulse of the universe within, and knows with absolute certainty his place in this world. If only he will remember this feeling, recapture the splendor and recall the comfort of feeling powerful in his own skin now that he has grown into a man.

DELIGHT IN THE DANCE

Dance with your feet filled with the fire and passion of you. Feel your rhythm. Sway your soul. Lift your arms like wings to the welcoming sky. Infuse your highest self into the movement. Spin your love. Twirl your testament. Share your moves. Dance your destiny.

HUMAN COMPASS

She's a wayward gypsy making her way down the path of unconvention. It's the whisper of the dream that spurs her onward, that beckons and invites action while holding and challenging her soul. She's a human compass pointing her way toward hope, toward peace, toward compassion, toward the ultimate destination... universal unconditional love, the lamp of light, the heart of home.

NO STRINGS ATTACHED

When he was a boy, he was told to be the strong one, bury his feelings, don't show emotions. Boys don't cry. For years he obediently wore that facade like a strait jacket. But he was a sensitive soul, a human Pinocchio, and try as he might he simply could not live society's lie. In a moment of sweet release, he chiseled away the wooden mask, cut the puppet strings, and that's the day he became a real man. These days he laughs until he cries.

SUCH IS LIFE

She wanted to pay tribute to the beauty of the world, but instead she paid her bills. She wanted to wash her feet in the ocean, but instead she washed the clothes. She wanted to run through an open field, but instead she ran the dishwasher. She wanted to sit and soak up the sun, but instead she soaked a mop and cleaned the floor.

She wanted to paint a beautiful landscape, but instead she painted her house. She wanted to scale to the top of a mountain, but instead she tackled a mountain of chores. She wanted to change the world, but instead she changed the sheets. She wanted to dream, to ponder, to write about the important things in life, but instead she lived its duty and practicality.

Today the house. Tomorrow the world.

BLESSED ARE THE UNCOMPLICATED

Blessed are the uncomplicated, the kind, the authentic folks who are true to themselves. Bravo to those who are unafraid to rise, be seen, and share their voice. Hurrah for those who embody integrity and exude honesty from the depth of their heart. Courageous are those who embrace freedom and are willing to expose their vulnerabilities, having removed their mask of protection revealing their soul's true radiant nature to the world. Let them be an inspiration and reminder to us all to live our intended beauty openly, honestly, joyfully and fearlessly.

CURVE BALLS

There are times when life throws us nothing but curve balls and we just keep swinging wondering if we will ever connect. During those moments we are invited to keep trying, to not abandon the game but change our stance, adjust how we look at life's pitch and tip our hat to humility. The game is ever changing. Sometimes we are the star and sometimes we sit on the sidelines appreciating the atmosphere, the people who cheer us on, the sunshine on the field, the emotions and feelings that bring a different nuance to each game day. Keep at it. Your moment will come. You'll hit it out of the park soon. The game of life is interactive. We show up and learn. We practice and perfect our skills. Sometimes we win. Sometimes we lose. But it is in the playing that we find our purpose. Swing away. Run home to you.

COURAGE *for Mom*

Courage is not just about making monumental, grand gestures or newsworthy conquests. For some, courage is enduring excruciating pain but getting out of bed anyway and putting one foot in front of the other despite the agony. For others, courage is moving beyond depression and choosing to see hope and possibility where they can. For those in recovery, courage is making the daily choice to honor sobriety. For those fighting cancer, courage is saying "life is so important to me that I will endure this chemo or radiation treatment one more time even though it is exhausting and difficult." For those who suffer traumatic injuries, courage is working with a body in its new normal despite the memories of a different, easier time. Courage for those with infertility is saying "I will keep trying despite the fact it hasn't happened yet, and I will have faith that I will be blessed with a child even if it takes longer, is not easy or happens in an unconventional way." Courage is taking the test one more time even though you have failed it before because you know this is your calling. Courage is taking care of a family member or friend who struggles with dementia or Alzheimer's even though there are moments that they don't recognize or know who you are. Courage is seeing the beauty in a gravely ill premature baby who probably won't survive another day.

Courage is going to work or school and putting on a brave face despite a disability that causes others to stare or judge. Courage is seeing the beauty in a scarred face. Courage is dating or trying marriage one more time after a bad divorce. Courage is leaving an abusive relationship despite years of weakened self-esteem. Courage is knowing this too shall pass and the next moment, hour, day and week will be different. Courage is having the faith that things will indeed shift and you will handle life as it comes.

All of these demonstrations of courage, hope, endurance and perseverance are indeed monumental and newsworthy conquests to those amazing souls who experience them.
Keep on keeping on!

SONG OF MY SOUL

Sometimes the song of my soul isn't exactly pitch perfect and I forget my words and mess up the melody. Fortunately, while my body may flake out, my soul comes with its very own auto-tune and all I have to do is go within and ask to receive. Magically, within a few moments I'm once again singing with confidence and clarity at the perfect time and in resonance with my passion.

SOUL OF A WARRIOR
for Kellie

Hers is the soul of warrior with
the voice of power meant to be
heard. Her emotions percolate
from the deepest place of her
being. Her wisdom beyond the
every day. While she likes
people, they both fascinate and
exhaust her. Her true escape,
her melodic mantra, courses
through her veins, charging her
pulsing hands in a stirring
vibration of creative expression.
Her beloved, her native drum is
her salvation, her rhythmic
connection to all that is, her
faithful companion whose song
is in sync with her beating
heart, an ecstatic expression of
genuine joy, her sounding cry
to a still waiting world.

ALL THAT I AM

All that I am, all that I have, I place into the light of your doorway. Bless me with your grace. Shower me with courage. Remind me that I am whole when I feel broken, that I am strong when I feel weak, that I am certain when I have doubt, and that I am worthy when I feel inconsequential. Show me the beauty of my eternal soul. Drench me in purposeful passion. Help me to transcend fear, to honor my purpose, to know the transformative power of love, and to live my life in timeless joy.

DEAR CINDERELLA

Keep those shoes on your feet, Cinderella. Stop running from your passion. Be kind to yourself. Release those who don't support you. Learn and leave situations that cause you despair. Appreciate the beauty of nature and laugh with your friends. Don't look outside of yourself for love or spend your day lost in longing. Love is always there and, like Prince Charming, it will show up when you are ready. Invite it in and let yourself receive. In the meantime, ask your Fairy Godmother of divinity to shower you with self-love and acceptance. Live every day the way you were meant to, rich in spirit and happiness. This is your best life and that's no fairy tale.

LIVE ANYWAY

Sometimes life gets in the way of living. Live anyway. Do it the best way you can. Honestly, wholeheartedly and with kindness and courage. Rest your body. Be gentle with your heart. Be open to the learning. Hold fast to the knowledge that you, like a beautiful star in the night sky, will once again emerge from the clouds and shine with renewed magnificence and splendor.

THE AWAKENING

She spent years trying desperately to fill the silent pauses of her life with noise, distraction, mindless chatter, anything to keep her from having a deep heart-to-mind conversation with herself.

And then the day came when her external wall of noise hit an overwhelming crescendo. The wall collapsed and her world fell silent around her.

Gradually, she learned to face her fears, to make peace with stillness, to forgive herself for her long absence. She had forgotten this place of solitude existed deep within her being.

In a brave moment, she opened the door to her soul, stepped inside, and stood in the silence of its welcoming. She listened and heard the glorious sound of her own voice. It was joined by beautiful messages of love and encouragement from the divine. This was her awakening.

Purposeful stillness has now become her best friend, her peaceful surrender, her amazing grace and the words she hears speak volumes.

BLAZE

Set your world on fire. Not because you want to burn. Not because you are cold. Do it because there is an ember of desire, of compassion, of love deep within your soul that simply will not be extinguished. Fuel your passion. Let it catch fire. Be your own bonfire of inspired action. Sear your soul in joy. Light your way.

JOY RIDE

Once more she reminded herself that it is okay to spontaneously enjoy her life, to be in the moment without the need to think about, research, plan and know every detail ahead of time. Life is an interactive adventure meant to be experienced utilizing all of the senses, a daily joyride of the heart and soul.

QUIET WHISPERS

You hold in your hands and
carry within your heart the quiet
whispers of your dreams.
Breathe life into them. Release
them from their time out so that
they can play in the world for
real. Fly your soul on wings of
creative imagination

LUNAR CALLING

Three a.m. shrouds me in eyes wide awake. Perhaps I sense the fullness of the moon and can't bear to miss its splendor, the raw whiteness of its beauty. Maybe it's a lunar calling, my invitation to dance along pathways unexplored during daylight, my insistent moon soul coaxing me to stroll once more along uncharted realms of my mystic self, to recall forgotten truths and memorize them with my heart until the sun's rays hit my body and I once again become immersed in the pull of busyness leaving me wanting for this peaceful exploration. I'm just a night owl, moon soul lass basking in the wee hours of a glorious moonlit moment. A wink at the moon and then rest will eclipse this from memory, but oh the sweet bliss until then.

GYPSY SOUL
for Victoria

She is a breath from heaven that lifts spirits by her genuine heartfelt compassion. A carefree gypsy soul with a heart of gold and a welcoming tent door who invites everyone to come in, stay awhile, relax and get real. Her passionate strength is engaging, her smile magnetic. Underneath lies a delicate soul who cries alone in tender moments, is moved by loving kindness and music from the soul, and deeply wounded by hatred, insincerity and deceit. She lives her truth proudly, honoring the gift that is her life. Unafraid to bear her scars to the world, she accepts the authenticity of imperfection in herself and others. Earth was surely blessed when angel winds blew her magical soul into this world.

LIGHTHOUSE OF HOPE
for Katie

She's been there, like a sunken ship languishing on the ocean floor, buried deep within the depths of addiction and pain. But she wasn't meant to be submerged for long. She's a survivor, a woman of faith and courage, determined to rise, to swim like a mermaid through her ocean of emotion, leaving her fear, shame and isolation behind in the wake of her past. She has arisen, surfaced and welcomes the sunrise of her soul each morning. In the evening, she bravely climbs the rocky hill of perseverance, taking one step at a time until at last she reaches the top, the reflective mirror of her lighthouse. She is a beautiful beacon, a shining example of hope, healing, resilience and recovery, lighting the way for other ships traveling in the dark of night.

GALAXY GIRL

She lives in an unconventional neighborhood located in a galaxy somewhere beyond life's proverbial box. Her preference is boldly drawing outside of life's lines with flamboyant flair and personal panache. No room for black and white or clear cut in her world, she's clearly a passionate plethora of pastels with divergent as her middle name. She changes her nail polish like her mind, quickly, instinctively and with style. A fun, free spirit, she's difficult to pin down, like lassoing the air, but keep trying. She's a brilliant butterfly who transmits ethereal beauty wherever she lands. Born during a parent's wish on a lucky star, she's genuine, the real deal, a one- of-a-kind who created and broke her own mold. On gray days, when you grow weary of life's monochrome, mundane, and predictability, take a rocket trip, look her up, her galaxy door is always open.

SIMPLICITY

She's an innocent child in woman's clothing tiptoeing blissfully along the edges of life's heaviness and pain. A pure spirit with an open heart who intuitively dances to a song no one else seems to hear. Love is her native language, compassionate grace stirs her soul. She appears naive, but her certainty comes from a higher source, her earthy wisdom grounded in unwavering faith. She's a flashlight in the dark, a nightlight when you're afraid. Her laughter soothes the sadness of your soul. She's passionate power in simplicity.

ABSTRACT

She is abstract, the unexpected
surprise who paints your life
differently. She gives irreverence
legitimacy. She blurs your exact
lines, keeps you guessing, and
colors depth to the in-between
places of your life. Love her for
her unconventionality. Keep her
because she makes your life
extraordinary.

NORTH WEST GIRL

for Megan

She lives in the land of eternal
sunshine, but longs for the familiarity
of pouring rain. She wears polos and
khakis, but misses the comfort of
fleece and sweatpants. She prefers
broken-in tennis shoes to a new pair
of flip flops. She's surrounded by
affluence and glitz, but she's a
practical, thrifty girl. Her spirit stirs
when the wind blows, reminding her
of fir trees in a fall storm. She's just a
Northwest girl living a California
world counting the days
till she's home.

She Chooses to Live Differently

She is ready for change, to imagine her life is now carefree, without the heavy responsibilities she's been holding onto. She chooses to live differently, releasing her worries and burdens on butterfly wings of freedom, letting go of all that weighs her down so her spirit and energy can at last soar as they are meant to. Joy beckons.

VOLCANIC EMERGENCE OF SELF
for Faith

"I'm fine" she replied but fine didn't begin to describe the volcano brewing beneath the surface of her soul. She was Vesuvius, a hotbed of churning, bubbling emotion. Her sweet smile masked a secret childhood of abuse, invalidation, and neglect. Her unspoken words were hot lava, desperately breaking through the crusty layers of impenetrable pain and fear in a courageous effort to rise to the surface and at last purge and free themselves from the angry pressure cooker within.

Truth appeared before her inviting her honest acceptance that life until now had been unkind to her. Wisdom spoke of the power of choice, change, and her body's call for action. Music lifted her spirits reminding her that authenticity is her theme song. Courage took her hand, helping her to break through the bounds of lonely isolation. Bravery asked her to share her self-awareness and learning with others, to appreciate the gift of her vulnerability. Freedom welcomed the expression of her feelings, the tears of cool cleansing. Finally, the lava of anger broke through her being, igniting a magnificent torch of compassionate forgiveness and self-healing.

No longer fine, she's much more. Beautiful, real and free, she's a resilient spring flower taking hold, firmly rooted on the hillside of life following the volcano of immense change.

YOU ARE ENOUGH

You are enough, as you are, in this moment. You have treasures within your soul as bright as the moon and stars. Open your arms and wrap them around you, welcoming your full, loving attention and intention. Thank your body for being with you, your soul for giving you purpose, your source for direction, assurance and guiding light. You are powerful, a capable, beautiful person with many gifts to embrace and share with this world. Let them comfort you on life's journey and remind you that even on gray, sad days, you are a light-filled vessel with amazing resources within you and divine and human support all around you. Believe and honor the love and the power of you. Awaken. Rise. Stand. Let your spirit soar as only you can.

ROLLING WITH THE RIVER

Our soul's river doesn't stop. We roll with
the changes. We coast. We float. Our
surface changes constantly as the
foundation under our feet falls away
encouraging our body's awareness and
focus on growth. Ride with me on life's
ever changing river. Float in wonder at
each moment's opportunity to evolve.
Don't pause too long or you'll dam up the
works. Be a pebble of purpose awash
in the glory of transition.

EXPLORING
THE EDGES

I'm about the edges, the empty spaces,
the extremes, the vibration, the touch,
the exquisite burn of full out exploration.
A neophyte of newness, I'm compelled by
love's longing to seek, to discover, to
carry pieces of scattered serendipity back
to center, to fill in the gaps of my
unknown, to experience the depth of
integration with a wanderer's wholeness
of being. If I'm not at my heart's door
when you knock, know that I'm on a
dreamer's quest, dancing my seeker self,
scouring the sky, gathering gemstones,
welcoming wisdom, marveling at mystical
moonbeams, polishing passion and
dusting the depth of my dreams. Soon I'll
be more home than you know.

BIG KID SANDBOX

Play me music from the old days, the kind with lots of drums that made me feel alive. Let me dance enthusiastically like a teenager back when nothing hurt. Don't cover your ears when you hear me joyfully sing some romantic torch song at the top of my lungs and slightly off key. Encourage my creativity. Applaud my unrealistic optimism. Have fun and laugh when I'm a clown, even if the circus already left town. Let my unconventional honest expression be heard. Open your heart to the unusual, the different, the all gray in our black and white world. There's lots of room to play and everybody's welcome in the big kid sandbox of life.

VI

Love, Emotions & Waterworks

On The Freeing of Tinkerbell

for Toni

She's a modern day Tinkerbell, a cute red-haired pixie
who longs for nothing more than a touch of color,
fantasy, and a little magic in her everyday world. On
the outside, she's all smiles, glitter and whimsy, but
beneath her childlike sparkle her life is no Disneyland.
She's a vulnerable flickering flame trapped in the dark
lantern of domestic violence and emotional abuse. Her
scars run deep, but she has a "happily ever after" spirit,
the heart of a survivor, and the courage to break free.
She desperately wants to live, but her voice is quiet
and her light is dim. She needs our society to believe in
her, to applaud her determination and strength of
character. Won't you please clap for her, loudly and
often? Believe she is real so she doesn't die. Lovingly
sprinkle her tired soul with pixie dust and help her
beautiful spirit to soar, to be free, to believe again.
Let the magic of her life begin.

ESSENCE OF YOU

With you there is no hiding, no pretense, no agenda, just pure, honest, vulnerable truth. My heart's carefully placed protections seem to disintegrate at the sound of your voice and my soul unapologetically tumbles in a free fall of rapture into your unsuspecting eyes. Long forgotten words of endearment flow like an emotional waterfall from my unrestrained lips. What can I do? I'm just so hopelessly lost in the essence of you.

Passionate Intoxication

I often miss the me I was in the blush
of our beginning, the one who drank
in every word you poured and lost
herself in the heady intoxication
of passion's foreplay.

Memory

You are a memory in the foggy mist
of my murky mind, a grinning ghost
picking the lock to the gate of my
soul, a "dare you to forget" trapped
in the forever of my dreams until I
turn on the light and you fade
quickly into the shadow
of my yesterday.

DECORATE YOUR BLAHS

She was a little down and tired of everything bugging her, so she decorated her blahs with ah's and moved on down the road to happiness.

No Accidents

There are no accidents just synchronicities! Open your heart to possibilities. Let your soul guide the way.

Timeline Of My Soul

Memories of you are forever etched on the timeline of my soul. Our spirits dance in joyful reunion whenever I close my eyes and disappear into the eternity of my heart.

Indie Hippie Warrior

She's got an indie hippie warrior vibe, a wild child, wind in her hair, guitar in hand, sister friend who owns the road and shares her gift in an unconventional, yet oh so compelling beat. Her heart swoons for the open road. Adventure stirs her sultry soul and music is her creative companion. She's a one-of-a-kind, free-spirited, you got to love her, songstress who doesn't think twice about what lies ahead because she's too busy rocking the day.

ODE TO CHILDHOOD

For a moment I want to remember life through my childlike eyes, with their whimsical youthful lenses of pure active imagination. I want to marvel unencumbered at a blade of grass, the movement of a bird, the height of a tree, the sound of the wind, how far away the clouds appear, truly appreciating their simple beauty without the adult need to mow, chop, shelter or protect. I want to look at an empty street sidewalk and see the hopscotch opportunity, the big cardboard box and see the fort, the doll or stuffed animal and feel the mystical bond believing in their transformative magical powers and soul healing potential. I want to play, to splash in mud puddles and roll in the wet grass and not worry about the mess. I want to color whatever I want, whenever I want, and not have to be exact or in the lines. I want to look at others with childlike innocence and truly admire their eyes, hair, and skin color, seeing their unique soul without adult-learned prejudice or judgment.

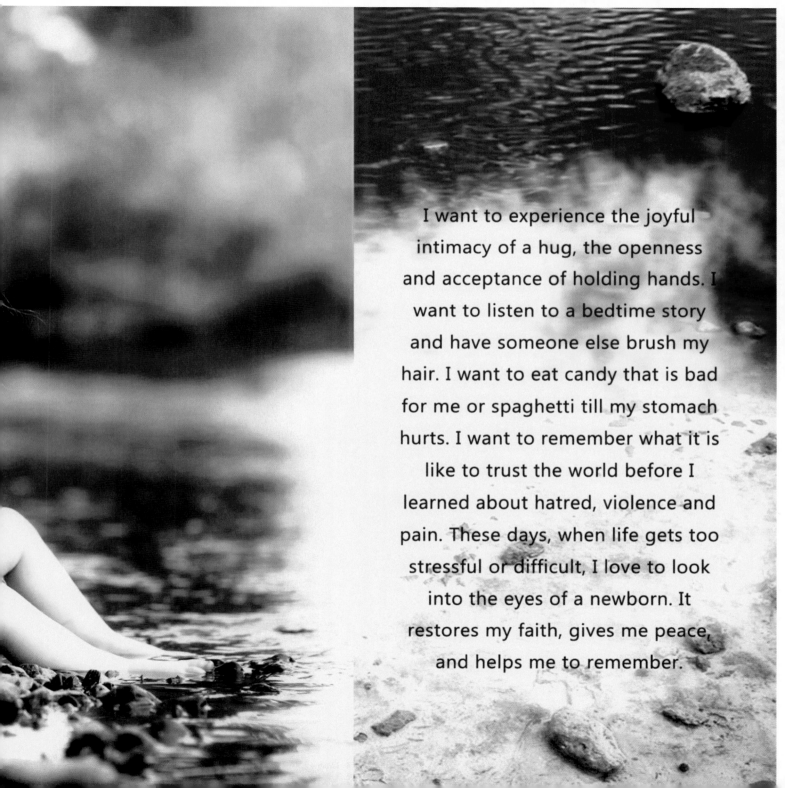

I want to experience the joyful intimacy of a hug, the openness and acceptance of holding hands. I want to listen to a bedtime story and have someone else brush my hair. I want to eat candy that is bad for me or spaghetti till my stomach hurts. I want to remember what it is like to trust the world before I learned about hatred, violence and pain. These days, when life gets too stressful or difficult, I love to look into the eyes of a newborn. It restores my faith, gives me peace, and helps me to remember.

PASSION PEN

Let the words appear on the blank journal in your mind. Then lovingly pen your passion.

RETROGRADE OF SOUL

The retrograde of her soul invited her to a little get together with her shadow self, the one she's always shunned and hidden away in the corner. It was enlightening to say the least. In fact, for all she's been taught in the daylight, it's her darkness that's earned her a master's degree in self-knowledge, wholeness and illumination.

BRING IT!

Bring it! Each moment is desire wrapped in destiny. You are the artist and life is your canvass. Create your choice. Color it with courage. Paint it with purpose. Persevere with passion. Dismiss denial. Accept the abstract of imperfection. You are a masterpiece of magnificence in the making. Bring it!

SOUL SURVIVOR

And it was in that riptide of pain, drowning in an ocean of fear and isolation, and going under one last time, that she finally saw her light, prayed to God for a life preserver, grabbed on tight, and swam for the salvation of her soul

AND THEN THERE WAS YOU

There are some things that defy explanation...the universe, miracles, and you coming into my life. While philosophers may ponder significance and scientists speculate on facts, the real truth is some things are simply meant to be and because of them we are blessed, grateful, and forever changed.

SOUL MATE
for dave

He's my warm place to land, my lamp in the dark, my calm in a chaotic world. His hazel eyes shine like translucent gems reflecting love and a depth of wordless, universal wisdom. His strength of character is chiseled by years of quiet integrity. He doesn't speak much, but when he does, his words affect great change. He's a peaceful soul, rooted like the trees he loves, happiest at home in the heart of nature with sunshine powering his soul. When he holds my hand, divine sparks of love charge my being, cares melt away, and all is right in the world.

Send Your Worries to the Stars

for Jason and Megan

My darling child, send your worries to the stars. Ask them to be blessed and polished with love and sent back to you in the form of beautiful confidence. There are times I won't be able to be with you, but close your eyes and feel my love wrap around you like a blanket. Know in your heart and soul that I have the greatest faith that you can do anything in this world. I'll be right there dancing on the winds of joy watching you grow into the radiant beauty that you are.

GOOSE-BUMP JOY

The times in my life when I have experienced the greatest sense of accomplishment, soul fulfillment and goose-bump joy have happened when I took a deep breath, risked leaving the so-called safety of fear and made a colossal leap of faith.

GRIEF IS A TIDAL WAVE

Grief is a tidal wave. It pours over our soul swallowing us whole, holding us suspended in a whirlpool of time, caught between the sweet memories of the past and life's new reality. During the storm, we are called simply to love, to bless and honor our loved ones on their journey, to know they are held in loving grace that their love for us, unlike the body, never dies. It is in the air we breathe surrounding us like a warm comforting blanket. We are meant to love ourselves, too, to be kind, to forgive, to listen to what we need to heal.

Our grief is in direct proportion to our capacity to love. There is no measure, no magic timeline for grief. It is a matter of forging ahead, bravely walking through the pain and loss, putting one foot in front of the other, until after a time the wave of emotion settles and a transformative peace washes over us and cleanses our soul. We come to terms and accept the power of a love that is much greater than us, one that is beyond the constraints of time, space, and body, a greater wholeness.

Although we continue to surf the waves, dipping in and out of the pain, we know in our heart that the universe's ocean is made richer because it contains and holds their love. They are always with us, surrounding us, lifting us, helping us to float and glide until at last we gently land on the shore. We stand on solid ground, recalling our larger purpose, going about the activities of the living, learning the lessons we are meant to, our loved ones' blessing until the universe sends for us, our wave appears, and we join as a ripple with those who came before us in the grand ocean of eternal and unconditional love. Until then, fill your soul with their love, seek peaceful understanding and remember your life has purpose and meaning. Honor the memory of your loved ones who have passed by living your life fully and well.

VII

River's End

WHAT IF

What if everything until now has been pretend, practice, a rehearsal. What if what really matters is this day, this opportunity, this moment. What if the slate is wiped clean and you can meet others starting now. What if all of the hurt, pain and grief of all of your yesterdays is lifted and held in divine grace. What if you had no more excuses, reasons, others to blame. What if today and every day is your birthday, your chance to greet life like a newborn, with fresh eyes. What if this is your last day, your celebration. What if everything you've lived has brought you to now and before you streams a loving light, a sacred invitation. What if your only choice is to step into your soul's glory.

BOUQUET

She reaches into the universe, gathering her scattered thoughts and runaway dreams, creatively arranging them into an exquisite bouquet of mindful self-love and places them before her as a beautiful centerpiece on the table of her life.

I CHOOSE TO FLY

I stand before the river of all that is, lift my arm
in the breeze and float my soul in appreciation
for each experience knowing it is growing my
soul. I look to the sky like a universal child, both
admiring and questioning. Sometimes I wonder
"why?" Often my why remains unanswered, a
spiritual mystery locked in love for another time
when there are no questions, just peaceful
knowing. I'm a seabird of time winging my way
across the changing landscape of life, soaking
in the sun, dipping my feet in the water, finding
shelter during storms, and resting in the
moonlight. Challenging events may ground me
for a time, but I will always find my way and
soar my soul in gratitude for all that is, knowing
there is purpose even if the way is unclear. Life
is mine and I choose to fly.

THE DANCE OF THE IN-BETWEEN

I dance happily in the in-between, where thought precedes action and creativity is birthed, the still point of life where alchemy stirs magic, the soul soars and transcendence rules. Let me walk forever in blissful awareness of my moments soon to be.

RETURNING HOME

Keep returning home to you and remember to leave your light on always.

AWAKENING

I've awakened from a deep sleep, the restful sabbatical of my body, the surrendering to the sublime stillness of my soul. The tired, scattered and lost pieces are alive, gathered and renewed. I feel confident in this place of powerful stirring, of beauty rising to the surface. The change I've waited for is happening now. I'm shifting, melding, becoming more me than I have ever been. This is my time, my amazing grace. I align with my path and purpose and welcome change with every breath of my being.

HAPPILY EVER AFTER

Your creative imagination contains your inspiration. Wave your soul's magic wand and create the life you've been dreaming of. Happily ever after is a choice. Begin!

WINGS
for dad

Believe your spirit can soar and the wings will appear!

LOVE'S LOGIC

And when someone asked her "why do you love him?" she could think of a thousand reasons, but could not articulate a single one. I just do, she said. And that's about as logical as love is.

FAITH ANSWERS

When I am in my deepest place of doubt, of questioning, of disbelief, that is when I look for a sign, an encouragement, the words I need to hear, a song verse or an angel to show me the way. Faith answers giving me hope just when I need it the most.

HAPPILY GROUNDED

for Leah

I'm happily grounded in the bliss of my moment, adrift in the delight of the dream. I take flight on wings of whimsy and wonder. Adventure beckons and opportunity bows inviting me to walk through the mist in the meadow of my yet to be, dance with destiny's desire and meld into the gala of my unfolding joy.

THE PATH

She let her heart guide her, trusting the pathway of her soul, the one of intuition, of higher purpose, of joyful anticipation, of faith despite uncertainty.
This has made all the difference.

ROCK OF THE RIVER
for Jennifer

She's a dry rock tossed into the river, ready for the grand waterfall of life to wash over her, to cleanse, to purge, to refresh, and to lovingly liven her soul. Awash with newness and potential, she begins again

BE HOME TO YOU

May each new road be one of
self-discovery, a reminder that the outer
world is a reflection of the exquisite
beauty that lies within and that all paths
lead to a homecoming of your soul.
Explore! Be home to you.

UNCHARTED JOY

Open your eyes to the new day with no
preconceived idea of what to expect.
Become one with potential. Explore life
with the innocence of a baby, the
curiosity of a toddler, the heart of a
volunteer, the wonder of a tourist, the
faith of a worshiper and the soul of a
gypsy. Live life new again. Explore
uncharted glory.

MOVING ON

She's ready to cross a bridge, to take flight, to forever leave the land of limbo, her self-imposed hell. She's done with doubt, finished with fear, and anxious for action. Tired of being a human mop, soaking up sorrow, paralyzed in pain, dredged in despair, and waterlogged in worry. She's wringing herself out, taking a risk, leaping for all she's worth into the open arms of faith. Her name is courage, her power is bravery, her heart is healing, and her soul is free.

JAR OF FEELINGS

She kept her emotions and feelings tightly contained, tucked away in a mason jar on life's pantry shelf. She was waiting for some perfect day when the stars were aligned and life was accommodating to open the jar. For years she was devoid of feelings, numbly going through the motion, dead to herself and to others. That perfect day just never seemed to come. Apparently, there's no expiration date on bottled feelings. After a time, she became emotionally anorexic, starved for her life, for her passion. In a moment of brave serendipity, she opened the lid and filled the empty places in her body. Raw, vulnerable, happy, sad, angry, fearful, passionate, she was back. It wasn't easy. Life, she decided, wasn't perfect, but the risk to feel was worth it. Her soul welcomed her back like a newborn baby and in the sky above, the stars formed an evening smile that made her cry happy tears of rediscovered joy.

About Jody

Jody Doty's prose, poetry and musings are inspired through daily meditation on the divine that every moment guides us on our journey. The words flow from the deep heart that beats within each of us. Her focus is on living your best life through the lens of the divine perspective with the hope that her words will speak to the reader's heart and soul, help to light a path and provide hope, encouragement and inspiration.

Jody resides in the beautiful woods of the Pacific Northwest with her husband Dave. She has two grown children, Jason and Megan.

Jody is known locally and internationally as "Jody Doty Soul Reader." She's a gifted "soul whisperer," clairvoyant-psychic-medium who has used her spiritual gifts for nearly two decades assisting others to recall their soul's essence, discover their divine purpose, promote mindfulness and facilitate a return to center, the place of inner peace and serenity.

She may be reached at www.jodydoty.com and via her Facebook pages: Jody Doty Soul Reader, Meditations and Musings by Jody Doty, and Poetry and Moon Soul Musings. She is also the internet radio host of Divine Explorations with Jody Doty on Blogtalkradio's Positive Transformation Network.

Jody is a Contributing Author to the Following Publications:

"Beyond the Loss: Breaking the Stigma of Suicide,"
Kellie Fitzgerald, IbbiLane Press, Nov. 2, 2015

"365 Ways to Connect With Your Soul,"
Jodi Chapman, DandiLove Unlimited, Nov. 17, 2015.

"365 Moments of Grace" Jodi Chapman,
DandiLove Unlimited, June 21, 2016.

"365 Life Shifts" Jodi Chapman,
DandiLove Unlimited, Release Date: Feb. 21, 2017.

ACKNOWLEDGMENT

If there are any typos, extra symbols, unrelated letters and unusually large gaps or spaces between words, I would like to extend a special acknowledgment to my three amused kitties, Izzy, Oscar and Emmy, for their exceptional dedication and assistance to this author by sharing their unique keyboarding prowess, skills and talent. I couldn't have done it without them.

Jody Doty captures your heart as she pulls you into her poetic world and heals you with her melodic words. The stars that are within her aura shine truth and forever you are transformed into a new and beautiful mind set. You know that she has written to your soul and the poem she delivers is for you. Her divine timing is always on cue. Jody brings her own spirit of earth and divinity into each and every reader's heart and mind where few are able to go without her guidance. If you want transformation and growth for a better life...read from the heart of an angel

Linda DeFeo

DIVINE
EXPLORATIONS &
Moon Soul
MUSINGS

A POETIC WANDERING
ALONG THE RIVER

IBBILANEPRESS.COM

IbbiLane
PRESS

Creative Design, Leah Frieday
Pathe Media, LLC
pathemagazine.com

Made in the USA
Monee, IL
06 February 2024

52967134R00086